FLY-ROD
CASTING

The Barnes Sports Library

This library of sports books covers fundamentals, techniques, coaching and playing hints and equipment, uniformly priced at $1.75. Leading coaches and players have written these volumes. Photographs and drawings illustrate techniques, equipment and play.

FLY-ROD
CASTING

TECHNIQUES
LURES
TACKLE

BY

J. EDSON LEONARD

ILLUSTRATED BY THE AUTHOR

A. S. BARNES and **COMPANY**
New York

DEDICATION

To Eric, with the hope that he may spend many happy
hours fishing with the fly rod in the years to come.

ACKNOWLEDGMENTS

My gratitude to Page for her usual and unstinting aid
and to Olga and Bill for their invaluable help.

PREFACE

Fly-rod casting demands a combination of timing and co-ordination. It is not difficult to become an accurate and accomplished caster if the start is made in the right direction. The right direction, in this instance, is the understanding of the fundamentals and mechanics of fly-rod casting and their practical use.

Experience is not always the best teacher, especially if that experience has been of a haphazard nature and acquired without giving much thought to the experience of others. A man may have a fly rod and catch fish with it for several years and still be a poor caster. Unconsciously he may have formed bad casting habits which have become so deeply rooted as to make their correction almost a matter of learning to cast over again.

If you observe well, you will notice that many fly fishermen have a seemingly limp, aimless style of casting and slap their casts on the water with no precision or delicacy whatever. Then occasionally you will notice one rod moving in perfect rhythm, its casts crisp and clean. The chances are its owner understands the simple mechanics of casting and uses them to advantage.

The ability to place the fly in a difficult-to-reach place is often measured by the weight of the creel at the end of the day, but casting technique is something more than mere accomplishment; it is as necessary as knowing how to hold a bat at the plate or how to correct a rifle sight for windage.

This book covers the use of the fly rod and fly-rod tackle, stressing the casting phase throughout. Tactics for specific fish are left out of account. Its primary purpose is to equip the newcomer with such information as to make the selection of tackle logical and simple, and to make the mechanics of casting with the fly rod easy to understand.

11

CONTENTS

FLY-ROD
CASTING

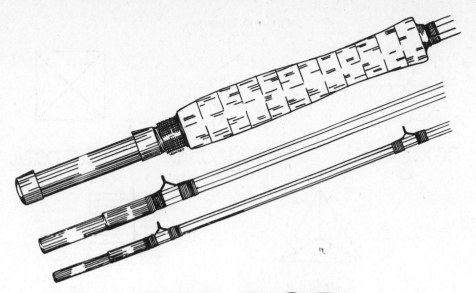

CHAPTER 1 THE ROD

Modern fly rods are made of Chinese Tonkin Cane, glass fiber, tubular steel, beryllium copper and certain other experimental materials. Really well-made cane rods have served their owners for years and such rods are hard to surpass. Nothing yet offered has surpassed the quality of the split cane rod made by a master craftsman.

New fishing techniques and the increased pursuit of salt-water fish by fly fishing have been responsible for the appearance of the other materials. Much can be said for their rot-proof and flexing qualities. Too, the recent resin impregnating of cane rods has been one of the greatest achievements in the rod-making field. A rod whose pores have been resin impregnated is the nearest approach to perfection.

CANE RODS

In the split-cane family there are a variety of forms of cross section. The generally accepted standard is the *hexagonal* type, consisting of six triangular sections. This type has been made for many years without modification. Recent years have marked the advent of less conventional cross sections supposedly based on mechanics. These are the *pentagonal*, which is a five-sided rod; the *square*, or *quadrate*, in which four triangles form a square; and the *triangular*, consisting of three triangles. Another type is the *laminated* stick, in which the cross section is square but composed of thin strips something like the leaves in a book. The square and laminated rod is one of exceptional snap and power. At the present time it is being developed in the smaller fly sizes and will bear watching. A square rod does have certain advantages mechanically but whether it will be accepted by the anglers remains to be seen.

17

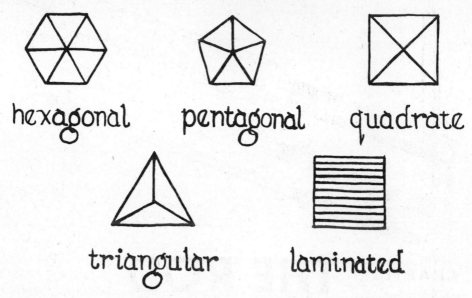

hexagonal   pentagonal   quadrate

triangular   laminated

Before considering the single- and double-built rods, it is well to understand something about the grain structure of the cane stalk itself. The outer areas (called the enamel) of the whole cane are denser than the inner areas, making it desirable to have the finished rod sections contain as much as possible of the denser outer parts. The whole cane is tubular and not unlike the skin of an orange, which is also denser and firmer toward the outside of the skin. Theoretically, therefore, a rod made up of the outer areas only will have more snap and power.

It is from this standpoint that the double-built rod is claimed to be superior. The double layers of cane in the illustration are cut from the outer shell only. Containing a minimum of less dense areas, they have closer grain structure.

The single-built rod, on the other hand, may contain areas from the center of the cane which are comparatively pithy. This is especially true with lower-price rods. The best single-built rods are made of sections cut from large-diameter whole cane, constructed from shallow cuts consisting chiefly of the strong, outer areas.

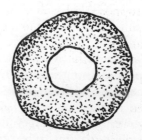

Some manufacturers have used a stainless steel wire core in the center of the rod to develop greater power. Certain of such cores have been successful. Rods of this sort are used mainly for rough fishing —big water, strong fish, heavy lines. Generally they are relegated to salmon and steelhead fishing.

GLASS-FIBER RODS

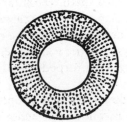

During the last decade much research has been done on compressed glass-fiber rods. Certain of these are semitransparent and solid, others opaque and tubular. It seems the opaque, tubular rods stand fishing pressures admirably. In many ways they compare with the hexagonal cane rod, but they possess a delicacy in the hand which is a pleasure, and withstand abuses that would smash a cane rod in a short time.

TUBULAR STEEL AND ALLOY RODS

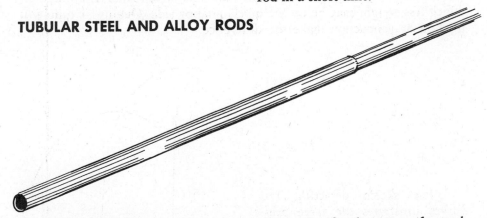

Great advancements have been made in the development of metal rods. In some cases these rods possess an unusual power which, until the caster becomes familiar with it, seems undesirable, but for long casts with heavy lines and flies, they are hard to beat. One of their main characteristics is the step-down design, in which the diameter of the rod decreases from the butt.

Whether the rod be of stainless steel or beryllium copper, its exterior is finished very similarly to that of the cane rod. Guides are wound on with nylon or silk; and ferrules, grasp, reel seat and tip are fitted as those of a cane rod. Metal fly rods are here to stay and may one day replace that beloved old favorite, the cane rod. I, for one, dread that day.

ROD CLASSIFICATIONS

Past experience and manufacturers' accepted standards may serve as a rule of thumb in the classification of rods. In reality, no strict standards as regards lengths and weights are reasonable, since the rod cannot be considered alone. Any rod will perform according to the limits which the line imposes on it. A class-A rod throughout, regardless of its price tag and trappings, will be a miserable thing with a line too light or too heavy. About the only effective comparison I can think of is putting a twenty-five-horsepower outboard motor on a tiny skiff or a small one-and-one-half horsepower on a thirty-foot cruiser. It just won't work.

Rods should not be pushed beyond their reasonable endurance limits. A single day astream may require several thousand complete casting cycles. Casting a line too heavy, or a lure, for that matter, will place the rod under extreme pressures. It cannot last long. Always seek the rodbuilder's recommendation as to line size, either level or tapered, or torpedo head. That, at least, is a sound starting point.

It is not intended by any means to set down here the proper rod for a particular fish or fishing condition. Keep in mind that actions are not necessarily determined by lengths and weights. One nine-foot rod of five ounces may have a soggy, weak action, another of the same length and an ounce less weight may be on the quick, snappy side. Quality of cane and method of production make the difference.

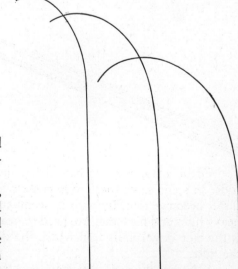

The sketch depicting rod curves illustrates the three principal bends found in most rods.

Wet-fly or, more accurately, soft-action rods have a gradual bend extending throughout the rod length, while fast-action rods have the bend mainly in the tip section and a little in the upper part of the second section.

Perhaps the most practical way to classify rods is to compare them with the size stream they will be used on and the size fish they will be expected to control. The most important consideration, however, is the length of line the rod will be required to cast, since casting saps the life from the rod far more than the handling of the fish.

Small, brook-trout streams call for only short rods; long ones would be out of place and difficult to handle. Therefore, think in the terms of lengths of seven and one-half to eight feet and weights of three to four ounces. Remember, however, that weights and lengths do not specify actions; they merely suggest possible actions. The lighter the rod, the more flexible, would seem a logical thought. But do not count on it completely.

Average small to medium trout streams do not require a rod of greater length. The same brook-trout rod will cover these streams admirably. However, if you want more delicacy and the chance to use longer leaders, you will do well to fish a rod about eight and one-half feet in length weighing four to four and one-half ounces.

Large trout streams containing deep holes, long runs and currents of complex nature demand a rod as long as the caster can handle comfortably. There are anglers who will dispute this statement, but the statement stands. Length in a rod gives the angler more control over his line, hence reduces the tendency toward drag. Furthermore, it makes long casts smoother, the lighting of the fly more delicate. Long rods need not be heavy; as a matter of fact, several concerns make nine-foot rods weighing less than four and three-quarter ounces.

If you fish for bass, you usually will be happy with a good nine-and-one-half-foot rod weighing no more than six ounces. If, however, you use surface bugs as big as hen's eggs, your rod should be about six and one-half to seven ounces. It is not unusual to fly fish for bass in really big waters where your rod has to work under the load of a long line and air-resistant lures. Under such circumstances you will find a ten-foot rod of seven ounces will reach places a rod only six inches shorter will not.

Steelhead rods take severe punishment due to the nature of steelhead waters. Streams of white water, fast runs, broad pools and churning eddies tax a rod to the limit. Casts must be extra long, flies large and leaders comparatively heavy. Too, the line is fished submerged. Under any condition, the rod must have reserve backbone. Steelheads did not get their name for nothing.

Salt-water fly rods resemble salmon rods as regards length and weight, although there is an increasing tendency toward rods of the lightest possible weight. Lighter rods are possible in the majority of cases, since the salt-water fish is usually hooked in open water or in water of sufficient area to permit a tolerable amount of running. If you wade, you will appreciate a long rod of at least nine and one-half feet to handle long casts. If you cast from a boat, the same rod or one a little shorter will do.

Remember, when you are hip or waist deep in water, the level of both forward and back casts will drop according to the depth you have waded. And if you don't think this affects the length of a cast, try it with rods of about equal strength and action but of different lengths. As an example, I recall one place on the Delaware where I had tried for several seasons to stretch a cast. Smallmouth would break just beyond the limit of my best casts. I was wading in water above my hips and using a nine-foot rod of excellent material weighing five and three-quarter ounces and equipped with a line of proper size. On a gamble, I built a ten-foot rod along the same lines as the nine footer and used the same line and reel. The difference was hardly believable because I was able to place the fly over the feeding bass with only ordinary effort. This longer rod would have been useless under most conditions, I might add.

So it all adds up to the conditions in your own fishing grounds.

SELECTING A ROD

It will pay to weigh the purchase of any fly rod carefully. Do not buy the first one you see. Know what kind of fishing you will do. You would hardly buy a three-ounce fly rod if you planned to fish for Northern Pike or Walleyes. And you would not do well using a salmon dry-fly rod on a brook-trout stream ten feet wide.

Furthermore, rods of the same category vary as to weight, action and length, due to quality, manufacturers' peculiarities and workmanship. Generally, they are designed and built to withstand, with a margin of safety, the strains and abuses peculiar to their class of fishing—but not all classes. Therefore, know at least where you plan to fish or, certainly, whether you plan to fish for trout, bass, salmon or panfish.

Consider your general build, your strength and temperament. If you have fine bones and a slender wrist, you must take them into account. What seems like a club to one man may be a wand to another. Actual fishing will prove this.

In other words, to say, "I wanna buy a trout rod," does not mean much unless you are thinking in terms of water, distance, *kind* of trout, the size of line and flies used. This does not mean you must buy a rod for every kind of trout in the book. On the contrary. But you should consider whether the fish will be a steelhead in a big, brawling river where you must shoot seventy- or eighty-foot casts, or a ten-inch brook trout in a trickle you could straddle.

Rods are generally arranged in three sections of equal length, although two-piece rods as long as ten feet over-all are gaining favor. Three sections make transportation of the rod more convenient but at the sacrifice of part of the rod's action. Perhaps this loss of efficiency is the main reason for the growing popularity of the two-piece rod. With only one ferrule to deaden the action, this rod will outperform the three-piecer. Naturally, the peak of performance is found in the rods having no ferrules at all. These are necessarily expensive and are best suited to hanging up in a permanent camp.

When you are buying a rod and can afford the extra cost, by all means buy the two-piece rod. It is true its handling in the car may be a trifle awkward due to length, but its performance at the stream will more than offset this inconvenience.

There are several key points which you should inspect before you buy a rod. Look at the node spacing. The node is the smoky spot that looks like a fine-grained knot. Each flat will have nodes in it. Since a node is that place where the ring on the whole cane has been ground flush, it is necessarily much weaker than the other parts of the strip. Therefore, nodes should be spaced apart, that is, no two should be side by side. The farther they are spaced the better. Soft or flat spots in the rod action result from nodes too close together.

Look at the seams. A well-made rod will appear to have no seams. Seams that can be seen will open shortly under casting pressures and normal moisture.

Reel seats can be made of many materials, including German silver, nickel-plated brass, anodized aluminum, plastic and hard wood. All are serviceable and choice is a matter of preference. Extra-lightweight reel seats of aluminum are often used on delicate dry-fly rods. Of greatest importance is the locking feature which secures the reel to the seat by a threaded clamp. Plain, slip-ring seats will sometimes let the reel fall from

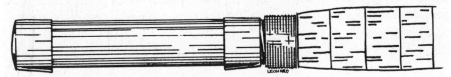

the rod—usually when a good fish is on. Another point often not examined is the width of the groove which receives the base of the reel. It is sometimes almost impossible to fasten a large-capacity reel to a reel seat with a narrow groove. Whenever possible select both your rod and reel at the same time and make certain that the reel seats itself well in the end cap and the threaded take-up or clamp.

The grasp of cork should accommodate the size of your hand. Some grasps are slightly tapered toward the front, others are cylindrical, and a few have various depressions such as a hollow for the thumb. Preference here is strictly personal. However, it is worth mentioning that grasps of large diameter are more tiresome than ones of small diameter.

Line guides are critical. Hardness is the first consideration. Tungsten steel and stainless steel are commonly used in the industry. A soft guide will soon become ridged and will begin to scuff the surface of the line, leaving it worthless. Weight, too, is a major consideration. Snake guides reduce weight to an absolute minimum, since they contain no rings as do

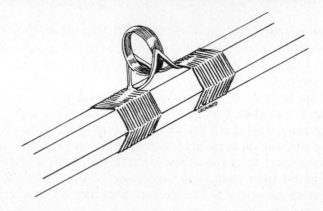

casting rod guides. These should be spaced closer together toward the rod tip. While there is no rule, it is more or less general practice to place four guides on the second section and five on the tip section. On the butt joint one large stripping guide, preferably a ring type, is located anywhere from immediately next to the ferrule to one quarter the length of the section from the ferrule. Salmon rods often have two ring guides on the butt section and proportionately more snake guides on the second and third sections.

Ferrules do not have to be expensive to be serviceable. But beware those long shouldered things that are more suitable as a child's flute than part of a fishing rod. Short, straight ferrules with serrated ends are un-

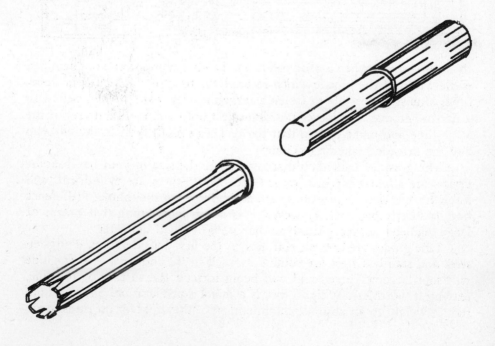

beatable. The mark of good rodmaking is often found in the fitting of the ferrules. Look for hand-rubbed spots on the male ferrule. They indicate matched pairs. Punch marks for alignment also show that the ferrule union is concentric with the rod. Pins are still sometimes used on some rods but are objectionable since they may have opened a seam at a very critical point—the end of the section.

Workmanship is not to be overlooked. Wrinkles and blobs in the varnish, poorly wound guides and trim bespeak inferior workmanship. Silk or nylon windings should be nearly transparent regardless of the color; since the varnish, due to its slow drying, penetrates the windings thoroughly. Color preservatives, which leave the windings opaque, prevent the varnish from penetrating to the rod stock. This will result in chipped and loose windings.

A good rod looks as if it was made with precision. Two of the finest rods I have, both nine-and-one-half-foot salmon dry-fly rods, were made well and finished beautifully, yet their list price was not what one would consider high by any means. Therefore, price is no real index of true quality. If you are fortunate enough to know a rodmaker, ask his advice about any particular rod. The chances are he will make it for a more reasonable price than you expect.

THE DETACHABLE BUTT

This is usually a feature of heavy bass rods and salmon dry-fly rods.

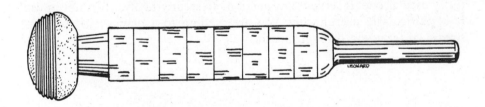

It is not used during casting since it would make for awkward handling, snarled line and tiring casts. Its main purpose is to furnish an extra grasp or a forearm rest while playing a long-fighting fish. A rubber button or cap is generally furnished on the end of the butt. One undesirable feature about the detachable butt is the ease with which it is lost or dropped. While casting, the angler keeps the detachable butt in his pocket; then, when a heavy fish is hooked, he pulls the butt from his pocket and slides it in place below the reel seat. Tying a piece of fly line near the rubber button and fastening the other end to the fishing jacket or belt is one means of preventing loss or damage of the butt.

THE FLY KEEPER

Most rods are equipped with a fly keeper located immediately in front of the cork grip. This is not a line guide, although it is sometimes incorrectly used as one. It serves one function: to secure the fly when not in use. It is particularly useful when you are wading to a new location of the stream or traveling through brush.

CHAPTER 2 THE REEL

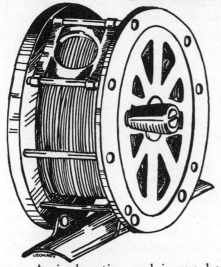

A fly reel seldom, if ever is used as a casting device. In nearly every case its primary purpose is the storing of line regardless of whether it is a single action of the simplest sort or an automatic having a spring-actuated retrieve. Sometimes fish are played directly from the reel, but generally by handling the line with the left hand.

A single-action reel is one having no gear train and consists of a narrow spool rotating on an axle. Such reels are quite elaborate in the higher price range, being equipped with ball bearings. However, one of the finest fly reels in my own possession is a simple, single-action type of seventy-five-yard capacity retailing for less than five dollars. Therefore it is advisable to consider more than the price tag when selecting a reel. Consider the italicized matters in any reel regardless of its price.

Shape. Ideally, the reel should be narrow and of sufficient diameter to have no "squat" appearance. Naturally, the larger the diameter the faster the line can be retrieved and the greater the capacity.

Capacity. There is nothing more irritating than a fly reel of insufficient line capacity. The line will pile and lodge and make casting miserable. It is better to use a reel too large than too small for the line. Since it is well to use line backing (ten- or fifteen-pound test casting line) under the fly line, try to choose a reel slightly larger than generally recommended.

One of the best examples is the Pfleuger Sal-Trout which has about everything necessary in a good serviceable fly reel. The following list of its line capacities is for enameled lines.

	SIZES—YARDS					
	H	G	F	E	D	C
#1554 pillar 13/16" 3½" plate	125	100	75	50	40	30
#1555 pillar 1⅛" 3½" plate	170	125	100	75	60	45

The capacities are for level lines. For tapered or torpedo head lines, the capacity can be increased due to the longer portion of smaller diameter. For example, an HCH line will occupy much less space than a level C, and a GBF still less than the HCH.

Ventilation. Although some reels are well made, attractive, and bear the label of quality, they have solid side plates which hinder ventilation of the line. Furthermore, they harbor heat which affects the line itself and the dressing used on it. Sometimes this destroys the line—at least leaves it sticky and unsuitable for smooth casting. It is well to select reels having plenty of open spaces in the side plates.

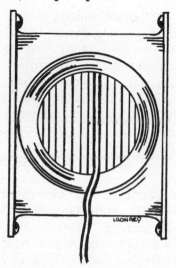

Line Guards. A line guard is an assurance of a minimum of line scuffing. It is a simple ring brazed or welded to the sides of the reel and serves as an outlet for the line to pass through. It prevents the line from doubling back when it is stripped quickly to increase the length of the cast.

Base. If you have ever ordered a reel without first checking the size of the reel seat on the rod, and found after trying to fasten it in place that it was too large in the base for the reel seat, you know it is good advice to look into the matter carefully before buying. In many cases, rods have reel seats of too small diameter for the reels one would like to use on them. Therefore, unless you are absolutely certain that the reel will fit, always try fitting the two first. It may save great disappointment.

An automatic reel is nothing more than a single-action having a spring retrieve, wound and preset. Such reels are somewhat heavier than the single action. The two types are the vertical and horizontal.

The former has its base on the circumference and looks like the single action.

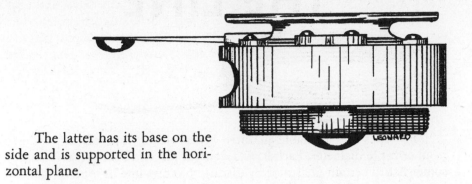

The latter has its base on the side and is supported in the horizontal plane.

The vertical is accepted more widely, mainly for its better balance. It is less difficult to become accustomed to since it is so like the single action.

Salmon reels are more involved mechanisms. They are called upon to serve more as mechanical things than trout- and bass-size fly reels. For this reason, their bearings are usually restricted to closer tolerances, their winding apparatus built for fast retrieve. Some of these reels are double multiplying to further speed the retrieve. However, there are few conditions when a single-action reel of sufficient line capacity is not adequate.

It is good policy to have at least two fly reels, a small one for general trout fishing, of sufficient size to accommodate thirty yards of HEH or HDH line over at least twenty-five yards of backing, and a large one which will hold thirty yards or more of GBF or similar line over at least fifty yards of backing. Backing is important since it reduces to a minimum the tendency of the line to remain coiled when stripped from the reel. It simply increases the size of the hub around which the line is wound. Too, it makes possible the running of a good fish beyond the limits of the casting line itself.

The fish and its environment will determine the reel you should use. If you will be fishing in small streams where fish will be restricted by the stream's architecture, you need not be concerned with large-capacity reels. However, if you will be tackling big, fast fish in water of unlimited nature, you will want to be well supplied with extra line. Provided it does not burden your rod or produce fatigue, a reel of large capacity is always welcome.

Some rods require heavy reels to feel right. Not so many years ago it was accepted practice to counterweight a fly rod by filling a hole drilled in the butt end with lead shot until a so-called balance was obtained. It is so much simpler to try various reels until you find one that makes the rod feel right in your hand.

CHAPTER 3 THE LINE

Fly lines are available in three types—level, tapered and torpedo head or triple diameter. Each has its rightful place in fishing but is limited somewhat to certain phases of fly casting. No one line or type of line can be said to be correct for all sorts of fly fishing.

THE LEVEL LINE

A level line is one having one diameter throughout its length. In the smaller sizes, level lines perform admirably for small-stream trout fishing and, in the hands of an old timer, will lay a dry fly on the water with delicacy. In the larger sizes, level lines, because of their heavy weight, are excellent for shore casting from a boat with the modern bass bugs.

THE TAPERED LINE

A tapered line is one having the last few feet on one or both ends smaller in diameter than the rest of the line. This makes for the utmost of delicacy in presenting a fly, since the thin or tip portion makes hardly any disturbance at all when it strikes the water. The ideal line-leader combination is one having the butt of the leader approximately the same diameter as the fine end of the tapered line. A gradual tapering throughout the line and leader to the fly results.

THE TORPEDO-HEAD LINE

A torpedo-head line is one having three diameters, the smallest at the end, the largest several feet from the end and the intermediate throughout the main body of the line. There are two principal advantages. First, the main part of the line, when appreciably smaller in diameter than the "head of the line," gives the entire line more velocity during the cast. The heavy head more or less "pulls" the trailing length. Yet, the fine tip permits the line to surface on the water with moderate disturbance. Second, more yards of casting line can be spooled on the reel, because the diameter of the main length is smaller than that of either a tapered or level line of equivalent size. This is especially desirable when steelhead, salmon and striped bass are fished for; these fish cannot be reached with the short casts common to the trout and bass fisherman.

LINE SIZE

Line sizes are often listed to suit rods of certain lengths and weights but, since the tensile strength of cane itself and the manner of constructing a rod are variable among manufacturers, these listings are merely representative at best. They can be used to establish a starting point; but you will need to increase or decrease the line size to suit your own rod and fishing. By all means, do not equip a rod with too heavy a line.

Even if the line feels perfect during casting it may ruin the rod in a very short time. One of the best guides to determine whether a line is too heavy is to follow the action of the pick-up. If the line tends to "stick" to the water, and the rod seems momentarily soggy and badly flexed, you can be certain that the line is too large. Try a smaller size.

FINISHES

Finishes for fly lines are limited almost entirely to the impregnating processes used to penetrate thoroughly by pressure or vacuum every strand of the line. This method is superior to surface coating, which soon wears away and leaves the line limp and flexible. A good line should have a noticeable stiffness which contributes greatly to well-rounded casting curves.

NYLON VS. SILK

For years pure-silk lines were the thing in fly casting. Recent years have proved the wonders of nylon which, in every department, is superior to the best silk line ever produced. It is mildew proof, has excellent resiliency—hence sufficient stiffness to produce good casting curves—and, with care, is nearly indestructible. However, when selecting your line, take into account that nylon line sizes should be slightly larger in diameter than silk lines, since silk is heavier. For example, an HEH silk line will compare with an HDH nylon line. This fact is often unmentioned over the counter. (The farther down the letter in the alphabet the smaller the diameter it designates.)

If you know the tackle salesman in your favorite sporting goods store, you may be able to induce him to let you try two or three lines. You should try a line before you purchase it.

The following table shows the approximate size nylon line for a rod of given length and weight. For silk lines decrease by one size, that is, for size E nylon, use size F silk; for HCH nylon tapered use HDH silk; and for GBF nylon, use HCF silk.

ROD	LEVEL	TAPER	TORPEDO
to 7½ ft.—under 4 oz.	E	HEH	not practical
7½ ft. to 8½ ft.—4½ oz.	E	HDH	HDG
8½ ft. to 9 ft.—4½ oz.	E	HDH	HDG
9 ft.—4½ to 5½ oz.	D	HCH	HCF
5¾ to 7 oz.	C	GBG	GBF
9½ ft.—6 oz.	D	HCH	HCF
over 6 oz.	C	GBG	GBF

THE LINE FOR YOU

One of the best ways to develop a triple-diameter or torpedo-head line is to splice your own. If you are a bass fisherman specializing in medium casts and large streamers or surface bugs, your line specifications will be different from the striped-bass angler handling very long casts and streamers and flies. Wind is an important factor. Casting the width of a canal-like river is no problem wind or no wind, but shooting a No. 2 streamer sixty-five to eighty feet in the marsh country where there are continuous breezes is a problem. Therefore, it is well to look into the matter of building up your line sizes to fit both your tackle and your style of fishing. Size G or F is usually satisfactory as the running or intermediate diameter. Start with that and try several feet of D, C or B spliced at the end. Do not be concerned with the tip yet. First find out the diameter of the line head which gives your rod the best power and the running line the best velocity. After you have established this, you can step down the head to the right-size tip diameter to suit the leader butt and the degree of delicacy you want.

All of this requires a little experimenting, but is worth it. A man who can cast where he would like to is apt to strike into more fish than is the man whose casts are beyond his control and shortened or misdirected by unco-operative gusts of wind.

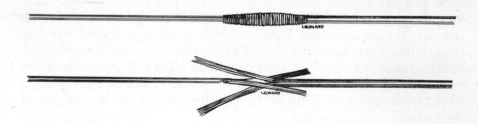

CARE OF LINES

Nylon lines require only minimum care. Ordinary paraffin is the best surface preserver and costs a few cents. Stretch the line between two posts and rub the paraffin thoroughly over the line. Then, with a dry, soft cloth, rub it briskly. This will give the line a polish.

Silk lines require more attention and are best treated with the special preparations made for them. These are packed in tubes, flat tins and bottles.

CHAPTER 4 THE LEADER

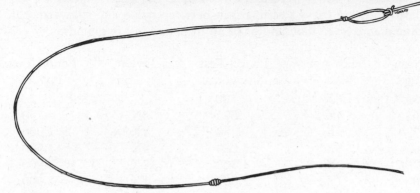

Leaders are less visible than lines, and the finer the leaders the less visible they become. Moreover, leaders, being light, are an aid to casting and increase the delicacy of the movement of the fly or lure. There is no doubt about it—with every foot you increase your leader you increase the chances of catching more fish.

LEVEL LEADERS

Level leaders have been useful for years for certain fishing conditions but are not ideal from the casting standpoint. Generally they are used in the smallest diameters for small brook fishing and frequently have dropper loops for the attachment of snelled flies. They are also suitable for streamer-fly and spinner fishing.

TAPERED LEADERS

Tapered leaders make for delicate presentation of a fly and should be used whenever possible, even with spinners and larger lures. One of the first considerations is the size of the fly with respect to the size of the leader tippet. Large flies, especially dry flies and full-hackled wet flies, tend to hold back during casting due to the air resistance. Therefore, it is advisable to keep the leader tippet and the fly in proportion.

NYLON VS. SILK

Leaders today are made principally of nylon and silkworm gut. The former has all of the ideal qualities expected of a leader and possesses a uniformity in both strength and diameter which is seldom found in the silkworm gut leader. Moreover, nylon does not require wetting before being tied while silkworm gut must be thoroughly soaked. However, it is a good idea to lubricate nylon knots before they are drawn tight by immersing the leader in water. Saliva is excellent for this purpose.

Silkworm gut is available in two types—natural and die drawn. There is inconsistency in the diameter of nearly all natural gut—flat spots and other irregularities—which is an invitation to rot and breakage. For this reason, die-drawn gut is preferred, especially in the smallest sizes.

The following list is a comparison between nylon and silkworm gut, including diameters in thousandths of an inch, and test in pounds.

Diameter .000 inch	Silkworm Gut	Pound Test Silkworm	Nylon	Pound Test Nylon
.0055	6X	.500	...	....
.006	5X	.625	5X	.750
.007	4X	.750	4X	1.000
.008	3X	1.000	3X	1.500
.009	2X	1.500	2X	2.000
.010	1X	2.000	1X	2.500
.011	0X	2.500	0X	3.250
.012	9/5	3.000	9/5	4.000
.013	8/5	3.500	8/5	....
.014	7/5	4.000	7/5	6.000
.015	6/5	4.750	6/5	8.000
.016	5/5	5.500	5/5	....
.017	4/5	6.250	4/5	10.000
.018	3/5	7.500	3/5	.....
.019	2/5	8.750	2/5	12.000
.020	1/5	10.000	...	.....
.021	...	.....	0/5	15.000
.023	...	.....	...	20.000

COLORS

The color of a leader is important only so far as it reduces visibility. A good leader with a minimum of sheen and a dull watery or olive-green hue is quite difficult for the fish to see.

KNOTS

As an aid to good casting, knots and the knowledge of how to use and tie them are important. Unfortunately, too few tackle concerns tie leaders with butts heavy enough to lend a smooth graduation from line tip to leader tip. Therefore, it is sometimes to advantage to snip off the loop of the leader, and tie a twenty-inch length of heavier material to the leader butt. Even better than tying is to splice the line tip and connect a two-foot length of heavy nylon to it, then fasten the leader butt to this line extension with a barrel knot. The first cast will prove the value of this arrangement, since there will be no abrupt change in diameters, hence no break in the curve or flow of the line.

And if you desire the peak of performance do not tie a loop knot in the end of your leader but fasten the line to the leader butt with the barrel knot. The barrel knot is tied like this:

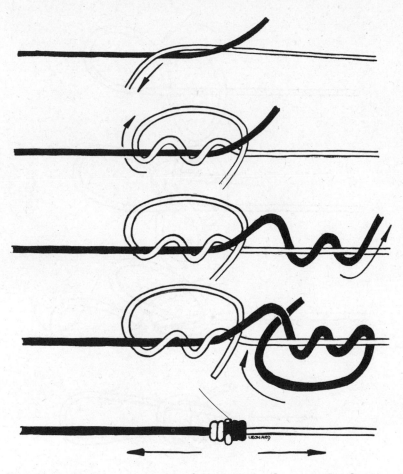

The Turle knot is unbeatable for tying the fly to the leader tip. One of the main advantages is that the direct draft on the fly leaves no right angles. The fly should always be in line with the leader. Otherwise, kinks and tangles will spoil many a cast. Try it like this.

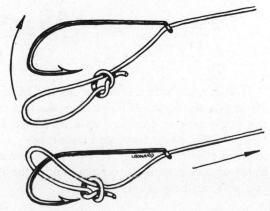

The conventional loop knot for leaders is tied this way.

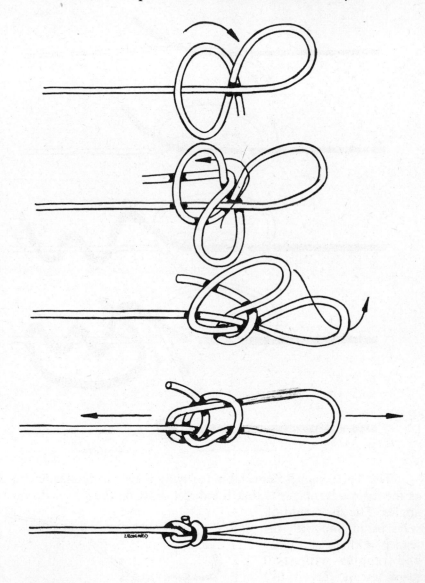

There are other knots of merit, other types for specific purposes. However, since snelled flies are certainly a thing of the past and one need not know how to tie loops in a leader to accommodate them, the **Turle** knot is sufficient for any end connection with the fly. The barrel knot is unparalleled for joining sections of material. The loop knot is ideal for butt end connections. If you can handle these knots quickly and accurately, you will need no others.

CHAPTER 5
FLY-ROD LURES

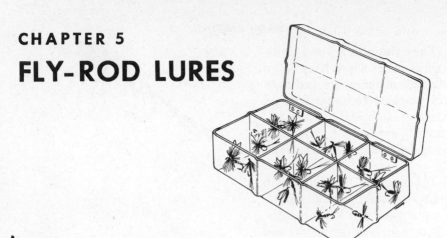

FLIES

In the past ten years fly-rod lures have become various and many. At one time there were three categories of flies; trout flies, bass flies and salmon flies. Adaptations of each of these in larger or smaller sizes for certain fish developed special types of flies, until today there are as many kinds of flies as there are fish.

For purposes of identification, we may classify flies into six types. The dry fly is one which, by virtue of its construction and oiling prior to use, floats on the surface. Its wings are usually upright, sometimes outstretched, its hackles somewhat bristly and at right angles to the body. This type includes the uprights, spent wings, hackles, spiders, fanwings, drakes and bivisibles, plus numerous variations of each.

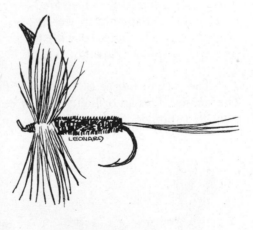

The wet fly is one which sinks because its materials are absorbent and offer no buoyancy. This style is fished below the surface at the depth required.

The nymph is a good imitation of an insect which lives below the surface of the water, but it requires singular techniques to be effective. It is generally sparse and natural in appearance, and even appears delicate to the human eye.

The *streamer* fly is tied with long hackles and is generally imitative of a minnow. Very realistic effects are possible with saddle and neck hackles and various shoulder combinations. Bass and trout wet flies of large size and salmon flies particularly are of this classification.

The *bucktail* is imitative of a minnow and is, perhaps, one of the most widely used underwater lures. It is most successful when tied sparse and is adaptable to wet-fly casting or, when equipped with a ring eye, to spinner casting.

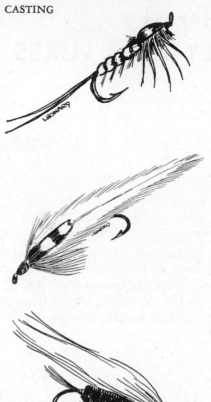

The surface bug is of large size, floats, and is used mostly for bass. The spinner fly is an ordinary wet fly equipped with a ring eye for attachment to a spinner.

SPINNERS

Spinners, which are as necessary to the fly-rod fisherman as to the plug caster, are of dozens of shapes and nearly as many finishes. It should be understood that only the smallest spinners are suitable for fly-rod fishing. Do not tax a rod beyond its reasonable limits by flailing the air with a spinner large enough for muskies. Good fly-rod spinners are easily recognized by their light-gauge metal, thin wire shafts and small couplings, swivels and lugs. It is usually safe to say that either single or double spinners size 00, 0 and 1 are not too heavy for fly-rod fishing with rods built for such service. But even though a spinner may be size 1 or 0, normally suitable for fly-rod fishing, if the gauge of the metal is so heavy as to make the spinning intermittent or the spinners hang like sinkers, it is useless.

While the following list is representative of most spinner forms and types, there are many others which have been developed over the past decade.

The *Standard Oval* is generally useful and has a medium radius of rotation. More spinners of this shape are used, perhaps, than any other.

The *Slim or Willow Leaf* is especially good with light flies and offers minimum water resistance since it revolves close to the shank of the hook.

The *Kidney* is one seldom seen today but has a good wobbling, revolving action. It is doubtful that its shape makes it superior to other shapes.

The *Fluted* possesses more light-refracting surfaces than plain blades and, for this reason, is effective when maximum light and flash are needed.

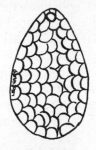

The *Hammered* is a truly great spinner and offers excellent flash plus scale-finish effects at slow speeds. In brass, it is the paragon of spinner blades.

The *June Bug* is an old favorite, having its distance from the shank controlled by a fixed arm and bearing. It revolves easily and works best at slowest retrieving speeds.

The *Propeller* is a fast, lightweight blade and revolves with the least possible effort. It does offer pick-up resistance and should be used in the smallest sizes with the fly rod.

Spinners fastened with split rings to swivels have the tendency, due to insufficient bearing areas, to twist the entire assembly, transmitting the twist up the leader, especially in fast water.

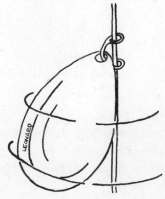

Spinners on lugs or hinges which revolve around a central shaft have very little tendency to twist the leader, hence are desirable for nearly all fishing conditions.

As an adjunct to the streamer or bucktail, the spinner is a necessary piece of equipment. I prefer this combination for everything including trout except when they are feeding on dry flies and nymphs.

Finishes have much to do with the success of spinners. There are times when nickel, for example, is too brilliant and will be more frightening than attractive to fish. Here brass (gold) is usually more effective. The color and clarity of the water, the brightness of the day and the fish themselves will determine whether nickel or brass spinners are better.

Copper is sometimes unusually effective. It does discolor more quickly than brass (nickel is consistently brilliant) but can be refurbished with any of the metal cleaners.

Painted spinners have been tried for many years with varying degrees of success. One stands out among all others—the small red and white June Bug. This is one of the best deep-water lures one can use and is especially liked by all members of the sunfish family which, of course, includes the basses.

One thing I have learned about spinner fishing which is almost indisputable is that if you blend the spinner with the streamer you are apt to catch more and better fish. For example, if you use small double gold spinners and a streamer of yellowish and gold color, or nickel spinners with white and silver streamers, your results will be better than when using combinations of opposite colors. I cannot account for this unless it may be that one complements the other and offers a more minnowlike appearance.

SPOONS

Whether a lure is a spoon or a spinner has been the cause for argument for years. It is generally conceded now, however, that if it spins, it is a spinner and if it darts and wobbles, it is a spoon.

Spoons which are consistent fishgetters have been developed for the fly rod during the past twenty years. New lightweight alloys have contributed much to this improvement, since weight is such an important consideration. Small, slim spoons with erratic, quick action are excellent for the majority of game fish, especially when light tackle is necessary to encourage strikes.

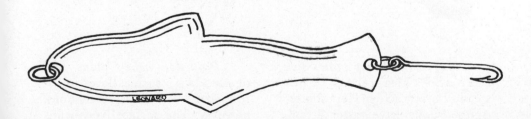

A minnow-shaped spoon imitates a small food fish and includes the tail, sometimes the dorsal fin. It is designed to dart and flutter, imitative of a scurrying minnow. Single hooks are superior to the treble or double hooks in every way. They hook deeper and more consistently.

A wobbler is designed to weave back and forth more slowly than the minnow type and is usually an elongated oval with the leader fastened to the smaller end. Wobblers should be equipped with single hooks.

The variety of features found in wobblers is almost endless. Some bodies are jointed, others have separate tails fastened by means of swivels. Sometimes even fins are attached and made to flutter quite realistically.

PLUGS

Small plugs play an important role for the fly-rod fisherman. They are effective mainly because they possess mechanical qualities not found in other lures. They float at rest and become animated when retrieved, enabling the angler to work them through areas not suited to other sinking lures.

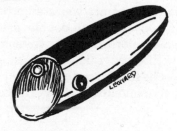

Hollow-head plugs run shallow and have an easy side-to-side swinging gait.

Poppers are strictly surface lures, being intended to create surface disturbance.

Plugs with diving plates dive deep and swim with a rather steady, choppy action. Here shorter plugs usually have faster action, while longer ones have a slower, easy motion.

Propeller - head plugs are nearly always surface lures in fly-rod sizes. There are exceptions, however. The surface type swims in a steady line, chopping up the water with its propellers.

Jointed plugs are usually designed as deeper-running lures and have a slightly faster, more wobbling motion than the solid-body plugs. They are somewhat heavier and must be handled with care.

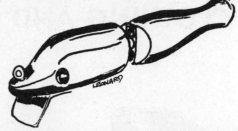

Colors are legion. All possible scale finishes are available as are the two-tone combinations. Metallic dust is sometimes applied in the lacquer. Plastics have offered uncanny realism to the plug field and give the lure a translucency before unobtainable.

CHAPTER 6
CLOTHING AND OTHER GEAR

BOOTS

Whether to wear boots or waders is usually a matter of personal choice. However, you will need boots for wading in small streams and generally for trout fishing. Boots of good quality differ chiefly in degree of snugness around the ankles. To a large extent, this is strictly a matter of preference. If your feet perspire freely, or you fish in hot weather, boots with snug ankles can be an abomination. They go on easily enough but sometimes require a team of mules to get them off. As for comfort when wading they are unbeatable. There is no chafing due to looseness and this is especially desirable when wading in soft-bottom streams. But if it ever were a matter of having to remove your boots in order to avoid drowning you would probably drown.

Boots with looseness around the ankles are generally more serviceable than others. While they may be slightly less comfortable, their ease of removal more than compensates for whatever minor disadvantages they may have. With the customary lace take-up below the knee the chafing caused by looseness is kept at a minimum. Furthermore, since they dry faster, they do not rot so fast as boots with snug ankles.

One good protection to boots is a pair of ordinary pants worn over them. They will deflect much of the rubbing and scuffing of everyday fishing.

WADERS

Waders seem to be divided between the stocking-foot and boot-foot type. There are obvious advantages in each. Boot-foot waders are heavier and require no auxiliary foot protection such as brogues or wading shoes used with the stocking-foot type. However, brogues usually have better traction than boot-feet, since they are equipped with hobs or felt soles. One of the principal disadvantages found in the stocking-foot wader is the collection of sand inside the top of the brogue worn over the wader foot, the sand causing punctures from abrasion.

Brogues are quite expensive and, while they are superior to any

44

substitute such as sneakers, work shoes or other makeshifts, they are not absolutely necessary. Ankle-high sneakers with heavy soles and strong toes are satisfactory at less than half the price of brogues.

SOCKS

Wool socks are almost mandatory regardless of the temperature. They absorb moisture and prevent the boots or waders from becoming soggy. White is the best color since there are no dyes to rub off on the feet. Blood poisoning which starts when an open crack in the foot absorbs a little dye is no rarity.

INSERTS

Inserts are sometimes sheepskin or tufted wool and resemble moccasins. The boots or waders must be larger in foot size to accommodate the inserts. They are perfection especially when the day's fishing requires several miles of walking and wading.

JACKETS

It is no longer necessary to wear a heavy canvas or duck fishing coat with sleeves. The modern jacket with six big pockets with flaps and shoulder suspenders is all that is necessary. The main thing is the pockets. These should be large enough to receive your largest fly boxes without splitting at the seams. Bellows pockets, or those with gussets are ideal.

For rain, a lightweight plastic rain shirt can be unfolded and slipped on and later removed. The rain jacket or shirt is transparent plastic and will fold into a remarkably small package. These jackets are not expensive; therefore the necessary renewal every few seasons is acceptable.

FLY BOXES

There is such a variety of containers for carrying flies and lures astream that it is confusing at times to ascertain what is best for practical use. Generally speaking, there are three kinds of fly carriers: the plastic box with several open compartments, the aluminum box with spring-catch lids covering each compartment or with single snaps for each fly; and the leather book having transparent leaves with a few absorbent drying pads.

The compartment boxes will accommodate either wet or dry flies since they do not crush the flies. If there is any advantage to the aluminum box with single compartments, each with a spring lid, it is the practicality of being able to open one compartment without disturbing the others. On a windy day this is something to think about. On the other hand, a plastic box affords complete visibility due to its transparency. This is a really important feature. The leather book is confined to the storing of wet flies since its leaves compress the fly.

Plastic tubes with screw-top covers are excellent for the storing of a few flies. If you are fortunate enough to have reduced the number of patterns you must carry astream, you can take three or four tubes, each containing one pattern of fly, and be well equipped. Furthermore, these light tubes float forever, and if one is dropped, it can be followed downstream and recovered.

LANDING NETS

The landing net for wading is necessarily different from the landing net for boat fishing. For the former, compactness, light weight and strength are the primary conditions; while in the case of the latter, length of reach, depth of bag and over-all strength are the primary conditions.

When you are stream or lake fishing the bag of your landing net will not have to be deeper than twenty inches. For larger fish use a gaff. However, when fishing from a boat you can use a very large net, with a larger bag and a handle as long as six feet.

Nets having elastic cords can be dangerous when you are moving through brush. The bag may catch on a limb and stretch the elastic cord enough to deliver a painful blow. It is far better to use a snap (similar to that found on a dog leash) fastened to the creel strap, preferably under the left arm. With this arrangement the left hand can remove the net rapidly, leaving the right hand free to handle the rod.

Folding nets are claimed to be fool-proof devices, but experience has proved above question that nets with solid frames are more practical. Why fiddle with unfolding a net when your mind should be on the fish you are about to net and the condition of your tackle?

Nylon bags are far superior to linen or cotton. Rot is the first consideration, here, if you are looking to several years of service from the net. Price is slightly higher.

CREELS AND BASKETS

There are many new interpretations of what a fish carrier should be, but few of these can surpass the old, standard willow basket for keeping fish in good condition. The main thing is to get a carrier large enough for the fish you expect to catch. A creel which has a complete bottom of leather is not necessarily more useful than one which has leather corner reinforcements. You want air circulation in any fish carrier, and won't get as much as you should if the bottom is covered with something which dresses up the creel at the expense of ventilation.

Some canvas creels or carriers with screen bottoms are useful. But there is no denying the fact that canvas does not admit much air. The same is true of the fly vests with the built-in canvas carriers. It is quite evident that air circulation is at an absolute minimum.

A good willow basket is light, sturdy and porous. It is about perfect for you when you become a wading fly fisherman, and makes a comfortable rest for the left elbow while you are casting.

CHAPTER 7
ASSEMBLING THE TACKLE

There is considerably more to assembling a rod and reel for fishing than merely putting it together and screwing the reel clamp in place. Always look over the rod sections before putting them together. Check the guide windings, the ferrules, the grasp and reel seat. A little attention of this sort will prevent unnecessary damages.

Wipe the male ferrule clean, then roll it through your hair. There is always just enough oil there to lubricate the ferrule sufficiently. Start with the tip section and attach it to the center section, using care that the guides are in alignment. Then attach the center section to the butt. Proceeding this way, you will seldom if ever accidentally step on any part of the rod.

The reel must seat well in the reel seat. Be sure that sufficient of the reel base extends under the hoods on the reel seat. Draw the screw-locking band up snug but not so tight as to make removal of the reel a major problem.

Whether the reel is attached as a left-hand or a right-hand wind will depend upon your own preference. Too, the position of a line guard will determine in which direction the reel must be placed. Naturally the line guard must face the stripping guide. Most reels having line guards are arranged for right-handed fishermen.

My own preference goes to the reel fastened so the crank or handle extends to the left. The reason is simple. Since I am a right-hand caster and do not like to reverse hands when playing a fish, I prefer to be able to take up line with the reel by cranking with my left hand. This arrangement makes it easy to unsnap the landing net with the left hand, as well. I have often thought that such a procedure has accounted for the landing of many fish that otherwise might have got away had I changed hands several times during the process of trying to keep things under control.

The same is true of the left-hand caster with the reel crank on the right. He can cast, handle line, play his fish and unsnap his landing net without changing hands once. This is valuable.

One disadvantage to a right-handed caster in having the reel mounted so the handle is on the left side is the looping of free line around the handles during some casts, since the right-hand caster invariably revolves the grasp slightly to his right.

Be sure you strip the line through *all* guides but *not* through the keeper ring above the grasp. Tip sections have more guides than do other sections, to keep the line close to the rod when the rod is flexed. Skipping one guide will cause the line to describe a straight line within the arc of the rod, thus placing excess bending stresses on the rod at that point.

The line should be lubricated thoroughly with any one of the accepted line dressings. Dressing improves casting efficiency and reduces drag on the rod during the pick-up from the water. It also prolongs the life of any line.

Leaders must be straight. To straighten nylon leaders, simply draw the leader through the fingers of the left hand. The coarser the leader the greater tendency it will have to curl. Silkworm gut leaders must be soaked to become pliable. However, these too should be drawn through the fingers to remove any tendency to curl.

Properly tie the fly to the leader tip, snip off the excess at the knot and you are ready to cast.

CHAPTER 8 THE GRIP

WRIST ALIGNMENT

Before considering the several types of grips and their most effective use, let us consider the importance of wrist alignment. It is all too often forgotten, although it should be one of the first things stressed. You cannot aim a rifle while looking in a direction different from that in which the rifle is pointed. Neither can you cast a fly line with any accuracy if your hand and wrist are not aligned with the plane through which the rod will pass. Therefore, you should point your thumb or some other part of your hand in the exact direction of your cast and guide the sweep of the rod with it.

To illustrate, pick up the rod in your right hand. Hold your wrist in a vertical plane (forearm horizontal and thumb up) and move the rod slowly back and forth. Notice that a full sweep of ninety degrees is easy with only a slight movement of the wrist. Now rotate the wrist into a horizontal plane, either to the left or right, and try to move the rod back and forth through ninety degrees. It will be awkward and uncomfortable. Therefore, it can be seen immediately that your wrist plays an important part in casting.

Generally, at least on smaller streams, the wrist is actually a fulcrum, the elbow held close to the ribs. If the wrist is not held vertically, it will tire quickly even with a four-ounce rod.

GRIPS IN GENERAL

There are more grips than one. Try all of them. One may be more satisfactory than another, according to the caster and the circumstances. However, the main point in using any particular grip is the amount of control it makes possible during the cast. Regardless of the position of the fingers, if the grip does not give the caster maximum control it should be forgotten and another used.

THE THUMB GRIP

Place the thumb on the top of the cork grip. Its leverage will mean more than you imagine. Furthermore, it will aim your cast and cause auto-

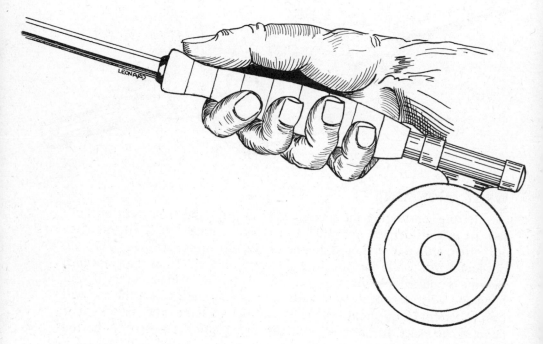

matic alignment from the wrist to the rod tip. Hold the rod firmly but without undue pressure. With the wrist always in that same vertical plane, lift the rod slowly by bending the wrist, until the tip is straight up. You will notice there is a tendency to relax the little and third fingers. And the larger in diameter the grasp, the greater is this tendency. This relaxation, however, helps on the forward cast. As the forward cast is started, the little and third fingers tighten, thus drawing the bottom of the grasp toward the wrist. This, of course, adds drive to the upper portion of the rod. Try it. With the rod held vertically, the little and third fingers relaxed, tighten your grip. Notice the slight snap of the rod butt rearward. This, coupled with the force in the top joint of the thumb, furnishes a surprising power on the forward cast.

Try this cast with the reel in place but no line through the line guides. Start with the rod parallel to the ground, directly to your front. Hold your arm comfortably against your side with the elbow close to your ribs. Bring your wrist up smartly, stopping with the rod exactly vertical. Then reverse the movement, squeezing firmly on the grip and pushing with the top thumb joint. Follow through until the rod is in a fully horizontal position.

THE FOREFINGER GRIP

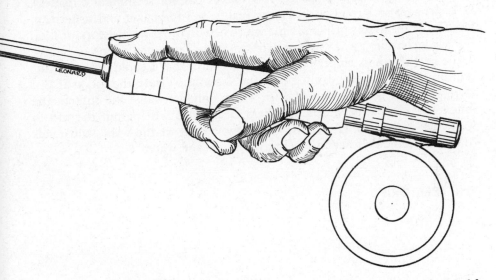

The forefinger grip is limited chiefly to backhand casts and should not be viewed as an alternate to the thumb grip. Some men find that it cramps the hand. The very fact that the wrist must be rolled out of alignment with the rod to cast with this grip makes it somewhat tiring. The forefinger on the top of the rod grasp does add some force to the forward cast, however.

THE TWO-FINGER GRIP

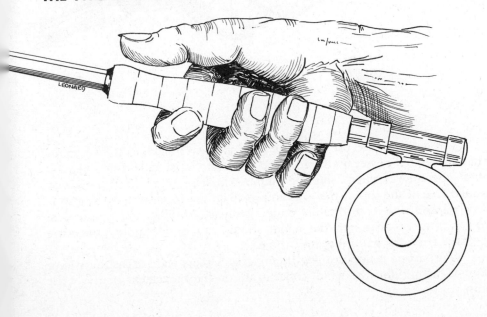

For using the lightest tackle, delicate flies and leaders on small trout streams, this grip is a pleasure and makes casting seemingly effortless. L. L. Schauer of Stroudsburg, Pennsylvania, ace rodmaker and fisherman, introduced me to this grip one time while he was ordering his stock of flies. He had a charming way of demonstrating it and got such a look in his eye while he wafted his empty hand back and forth that I could hear the current of the Brodheads gurgling past the showcase. Grasp the rod as if you were going to use the thumb grip. Then simply remove the thumb, the index and little fingers, holding them clear. This will permit the rod to rock back and forth with the slightest movement of the wrist, and tends toward extreme delicacy in placing the fly on the water.

THE FREE GRIP

This is the grip to use when casts are short and tackle is light, requiring only limited power on the forward cast. The wrist is held in a vertical plane, the same as when using the thumb grip. The thumb itself, however, is held free of the top of the grip and rests on the forefinger. This grip is very relaxed and comfortable under ordinary trout-stream conditions. Power casts, or casts into the wind, should not be attempted since the leverage from the hand just isn't there.

Wrist action is important with any grip. Unless you are casting a long line, or casting into the wind, concentrate on the movement of the wrist only.

THE WRIST AS THE FULCRUM

The wrist joint becomes the fulcrum in ordinary trout-stream fishing. The larger percentage of the average fly fisherman's casting will be done on this basis.

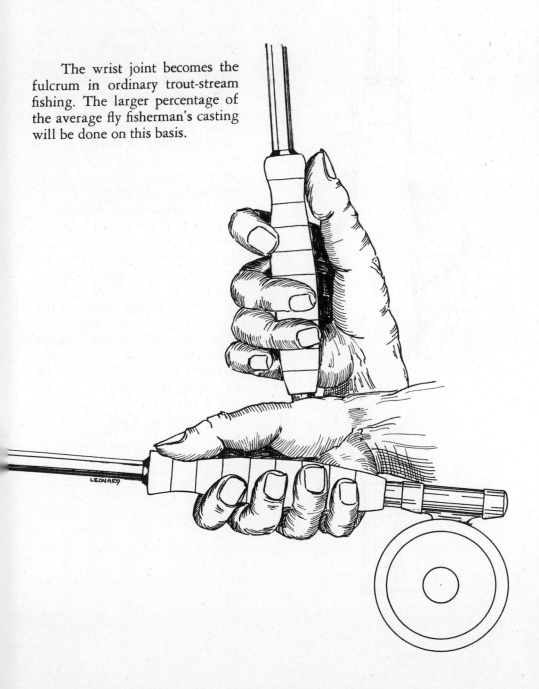

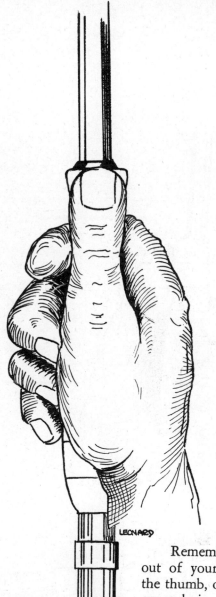

Circumstances alter the mechanics of casting. Deep-water wading, wind, distance and terminal tackle sometimes demand more casting power than the wrist can provide. Then the forearm comes into use. The elbow becomes the fulcrum and the wrist is held stiff in such a manner that the rod and entire forearm become a unit. There is a certain amount of awkwardness with this arrangement at first, until timing the back cast and putting pressure into the forward cast become automatic.

Hurried and erratic attempts to achieve distance will only kill the cast. A definite, measured rhythm is necessary to keep the line curve well overhead, incurring a minimum of shallow "hooks" in the ends of the back and forward stages of each cast. Begin with slow and deliberate movement even though it may seem awkward and too slow at the outset. Allow sufficient time for the line to straighten. Then, gradually increase casting speed.

Remember, to get the most out of your casting efforts keep the thumb, or at least the hand in general, in the same plane with the rod.

CHAPTER 9 THE CAST

Casting is simply rhythm and timing, made possible by a rod, reel and line well suited to one another. Notice the word "balanced" was not used. "Balanced" is a vague word when used in connection with fishing tackle. A reel cannot balance a rod; it merely adds weight to the bottom of the rod and makes the rod feel better to the hand. If you "balance" a rod by fastening to it a reel of sufficient weight to cause equal distribution of weight at a point, say, immediately in front of the grasp, what becomes of that "balance" when half the line is stripped from the reel and extended beyond the rod tip, as when casting? So forget about the impossible-to-attain delicacies of balance. Flow of power and co-ordinated movements during casting are far more important.

It is generally safe to figure that a reel of sufficient capacity for the line which draws peak performance from the rod will be of the right weight to make the rod feel correct.

THE MECHANICS OF CASTING

Before examining the characteristics of any particular style of casting, let us first look to the general mechanics of casting itself. You should know these since any cast is and must be based on these principles.

First, a single cast consists of three phases: the *pick-up*, the *pause*, the *forward cast*. Each of these may be modified somewhat to adapt a special kind of cast to a specific fishing condition; however, in nearly every case, the three phases are primarily the same.

Assume your gear is proper and working in full harmony. You have greased your line to reduce friction against the line guides and are ready to start casting. Draw about two rod lengths of line through the tip guide.

Holding the rod directly to your front with your wrist in a vertical plane, your thumb on top of the grasp, swing the rod horizontally from left to right so that you may observe the entire business. Watch the flexing of the rod, the curve of the line. With the left hand strip out two more rod lengths of line—gradually of course—and observe the greater curving of line, the deeper bend in the rod. Intentionally, do something wrong here to prove a point. Accelerate the sweeps of the rod. Notice that almost at once the rhythm of the rod and line is broken. The rod will reverse its movement before the line has completed its looping curve. This is a simple way to illustrate the importance of rhythm and timing. And the longer the cast, the more important this rhythm and timing are. Profit by the incorrect cast you have just made, remembering to let the line dictate to the rod.

THE OVERHEAD CAST

It is a simple step now to the Overhead Cast, used more than any other because it is easily mastered and its uses are seldom limited in actual fishing. Begin again with two rod lengths of line stripped from the rod tip, the rod to your front, the wrist in a vertical plane and the elbow next to your ribs. Instead of moving the rod in a plane parallel to the ground, move it in a vertical plane, casting

back and forth over your right shoulder. Again strip out about two more rod lengths from the tip of the rod and try to cast back and forth as smoothly as possible. The chances are that you have bungled the forward cast by this time. If you have, the reason is pretty obvious. Because you could not see what the line was doing behind you, you instinctively started the forward cast before the back cast had completed its unlooping. In other words, the premature forward sweep of your rod had little to pull with it, since the line loop remaining from the back cast was probably directly overhead. Therefore, and for the time being only, turn your head with each back cast, and follow it through by watching its unlooping behind you. This is not good practice, but will prove useful to you while you become familiar with the rhythm of casting. Later, you will not be at all aware of waiting for the back cast and will time your forward cast automatically.

Now for a little refinement of what you have already accomplished. It was mentioned previously that there were three phases in casting: the *pick-up,* the *pause,* the *forward cast.* Let's consider each one individually to see how it affects the other two.

THE PICK-UP

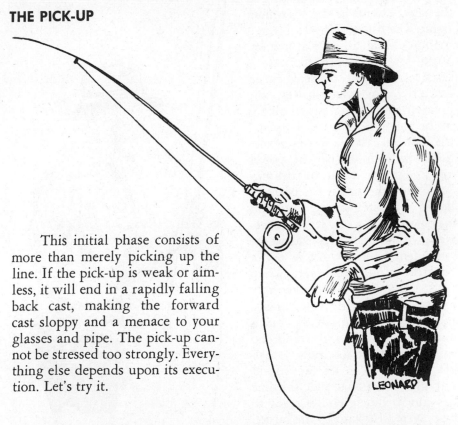

This initial phase consists of more than merely picking up the line. If the pick-up is weak or aimless, it will end in a rapidly falling back cast, making the forward cast sloppy and a menace to your glasses and pipe. The pick-up cannot be stressed too strongly. Everything else depends upon its execution. Let's try it.

Extend three rod lengths of line to your front. Using the thumb grip, bring the rod upward with increasingly brisk movement of the hand and stop when the rod is in the fully vertical position. Follow the line with your eyes and notice how cleanly it flows from a deep loop into a straight line to the rear. Vary the briskness with which you pick up the line and you will notice a proportionately weak or strong flow of line to the rear. A slow pick-up will mean a slow uncoiling of line during the pause and a low back cast from which to start the forward cast, which is to be avoided.

Generally, a brisk, clean pick-up ends in a smooth-flowing forward cast.

THE PAUSE

This second phase has one purpose: to let the line, moving to the rear, extend to the maximum point. The pause, in itself, is not a motion, it is an absence of motion. With few exceptions the cast is satisfactory if the pause is timed correctly. For that matter, the greatest part timing has to play is in the pause. Both the pick-up and the forward cast are phases of motion which emphasize the power applied more than of timing. Sometimes the pause has been reduced to a system of counting; this may be useful to a degree, especially if the casts are exactly the same length and wind is not a consideration. However, when casts on the stream and river vary anywhere from little more than a rod length to almost the maximum that a rod will stand, no single method of counting is feasible. It is better to let the line itself give the signal that the line has run its course and is ready to be powered forward to the target.

Therefore, it is reasonable to wait for the slight but unmistakable tug of the line at the end of the back cast. This tug comes some fractional part of a second later than expected, largely because you cannot see what is going on behind you. But if you wait for that tug, then bring your rod forward crisply with control, the line will roll out at the proper height and with the least effort. A tail wind will reduce the power of the tug by slowing the rearward movement of the line. How to overcome this condition will be described a little later.

It should be pointed out here that the common tendency is to let the rod fall too far beyond the vertical. By all means check this before the habit is firmly rooted. Each degree that the rod falls beyond the vertical permits the trailing line to drop a little closer to the ground to become tangled with brush or grass. So be watchful that you begin the pause with the rod as close to vertical as you can estimate.

Long rods—rods nine and a half feet or longer—help keep the back cast high. Therefore, under circumstances where the greatest possible rod sweep is desired, these longer rods can be dropped beyond the vertical without too much concern for the height of the back cast.

THE FORWARD CAST

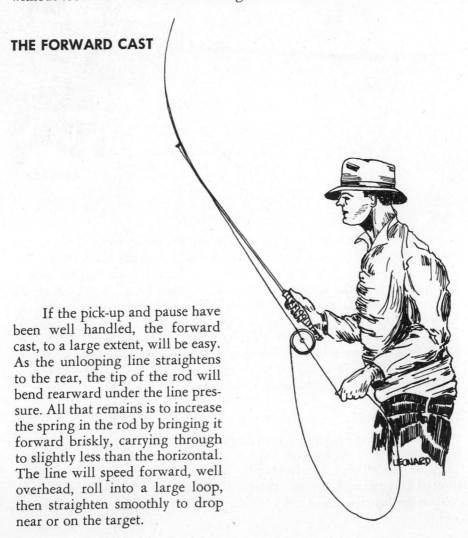

If the pick-up and pause have been well handled, the forward cast, to a large extent, will be easy. As the unlooping line straightens to the rear, the tip of the rod will bend rearward under the line pressure. All that remains is to increase the spring in the rod by bringing it forward briskly, carrying through to slightly less than the horizontal. The line will speed forward, well overhead, roll into a large loop, then straighten smoothly to drop near or on the target.

You can see that the maximum power will be lost if you start the forward cast too soon, since casting power depends almost entirely upon rod flexure, as started by the lengthening of the line to the rear during the pause.

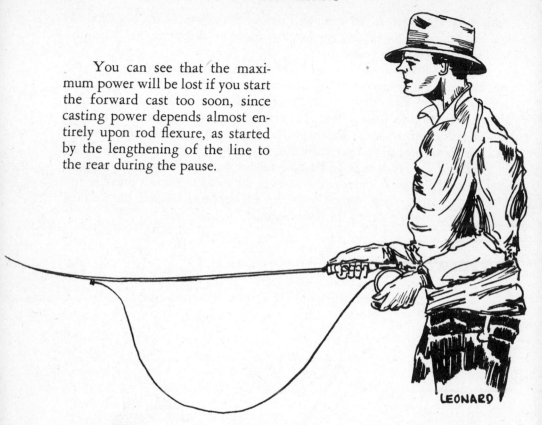

LEONARD

For the present, concentrate on the rhythm experienced through the three phases. If you once become familiar with sensing this rhythm, the length of the cast will take care of itself. Too, accuracy will become almost automatic as determined by the crispness of your pick-up, the length of your pause, and the clean, well-aimed delivery of your forward cast. So far as lassoing a dime at sixty feet is concerned, forget it. Entirely too much emphasis is placed on this nonsense. And fishing will prove it. If you can place a fly within a foot of where you aim, you are an exception. A tiny gust of air anywhere along the line's route can deflect the cast that much. Look to smoothness and avoidance of fatigue.

THE FALSE CAST

It is frequently necessary to measure casts by sensing with two or three trial casts kept in the air over the target. Such casts are called false casts. They are further useful in freeing the dry fly of surplus moisture. Two or three flights through the air will eliminate most of the moisture which collects on hackles. False casts are one method used to produce desired line length.

THE SIDE CAST

The Side Cast is a close companion to the Overhead Cast. Hardly does the fishing day pass when these two casts are not used with alternate frequency. One of the main reasons for using the Side Cast is to avoid low-hanging brush. This employs the same fundamentals as the Overhead Cast, but the rod moves through a horizontal plane. A greater degree of delicacy is attainable with the Side Cast, particularly when casts are relatively short. Long casts are difficult with the Side Cast, because the back cast must be so low.

Perhaps the main achievement of a successful Side Cast is the placement of the fly under obstructions which would prevent the use of any other cast. Refinements in presenting the fly to the fish are possible too, by casting right and left loops in order to overcome drag. These refinements will be explained later.

It seems to be common practice to let the reel hang vertically and the rod remain the same as when making the Overhead or other casts. There is one disadvantage. The wrist is revolved out of alignment.

After checking and trying the two possible grips for the Side Cast, I have the best reasons to believe that it is better to grasp the rod as when making the Overhead Cast and bend the wrist, so that the hand, rod and reel move in a horizontal plane. This will allow the rod to flex almost exactly as it does during the Overhead Cast.

THE ROLL CAST

This cast is best used when high obstructions prevent a back cast. You will frequently meet the condition where you must stand immediately in front of a high rock shelf or cluster of trees. The Roll Cast, while not the easiest form to control, will place the fly with sufficient accuracy and delicacy to reach rising fish otherwise unapproachable. If your particular fishing water consists of streams heavily bordered, you will do well to practice the Roll Cast.

One of the best ways to illustrate the cast is to pick up a length of rope of, say, twenty feet and flip a large loop in it. Notice that the remaining portion will follow or try to follow the loop. Now substitute a rod for your arm and line for the rope.

First strip about twenty-five feet of line from the rod tip and make a simple cast in order to get the line to your front. Now draw the rod slowly to a vertical position, at the same time extending the arm full length vertically over the head. This will produce a sag in the line from the rod tip, which is important. This sagging part of the line is the impetus behind the cast itself.

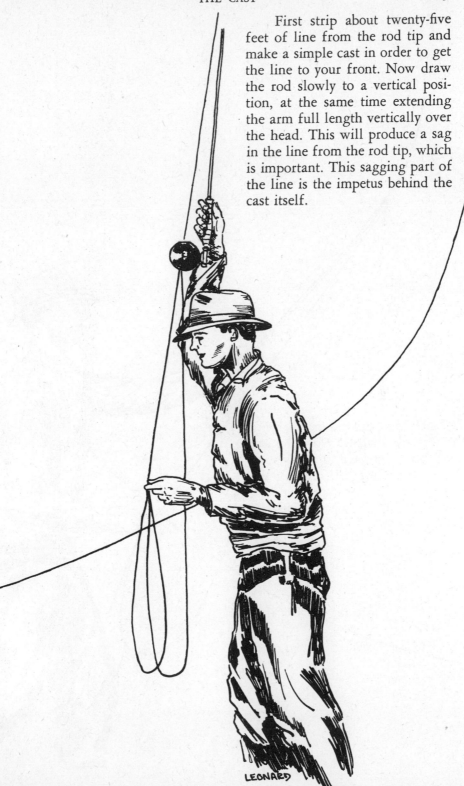

LEONARD

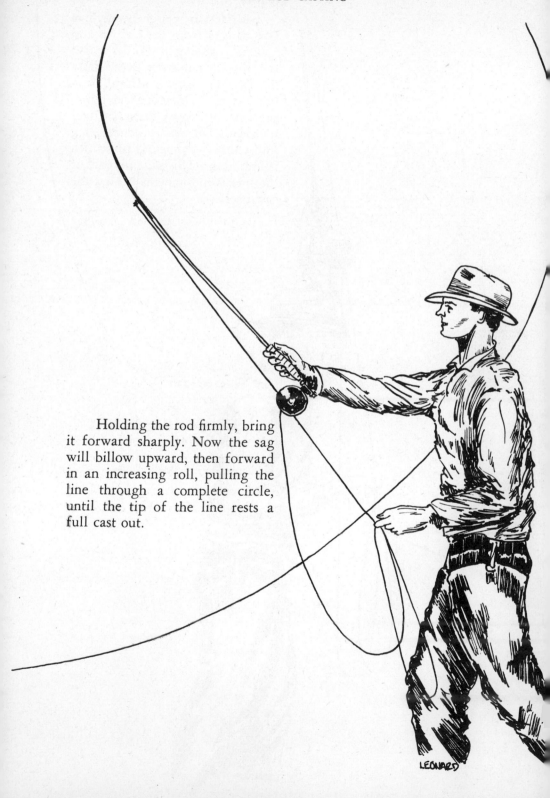

Holding the rod firmly, bring it forward sharply. Now the sag will billow upward, then forward in an increasing roll, pulling the line through a complete circle, until the tip of the line rests a full cast out.

Draw the arm back to the at-rest position.

In actual casting, the described motions are continuous in a flow of power. The gradual lifting of the rod and rolling out of the line are one sweeping action. Any interruption or pause will destroy the widening roll in the line.

THE BACKHAND CAST

BANK TO REAR

OBSTRUCTIONS TO RIGHT OF SHOULDER

There are times when you must wade on the right side of the stream with your back close to the bank, and the Overhead and Side Casts are all but impossible. During such times, you will have to make Backhand Casts. They may seem awkward at first. However, if you consider the backhand as similar to a Side Cast but performed parallel to your front, you should have little difficulty.

Always face across the stream, or with your back parallel to the bank. Naturally you will be casting to your right or upstream, so what would normally be a forward cast will now become a back cast and a back cast the forward cast.

A simple way to begin the Backhand Cast is to look to your left or downstream and cast exactly as you would when using the Side Cast, then after the line has made its last false cast, turn your head to the right, toward the target, and follow through with the usual final sweep of the rod.

There are variations of this cast, one being a sort of overhead cast handled over the left shoulder, the body facing upstream toward the target.

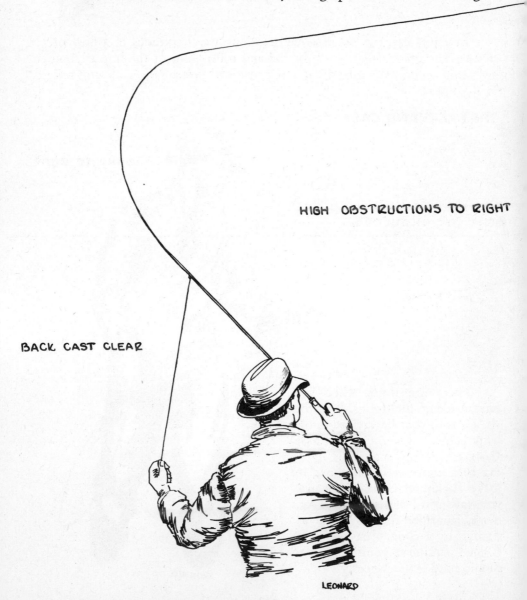

HIGH OBSTRUCTIONS TO RIGHT

BACK CAST CLEAR

LEONARD

This, however, creates tension and becomes tiring in a very short time. It is possible to obtain more power on the forward cast at the sacrifice of accuracy. Incidentally, this is one case where the forefinger grip is not only useful but necessary, since the wrist cannot be revolved into a position to compare with its position during ordinary overhead casting. This cast can be dropped to the horizontal position when obstructions are overhead.

TARGET TO FRONT

OBSTRUCTIONS LOW OVERHEAD

LEONARD

THE VERTICAL OR HIGH BANK CAST

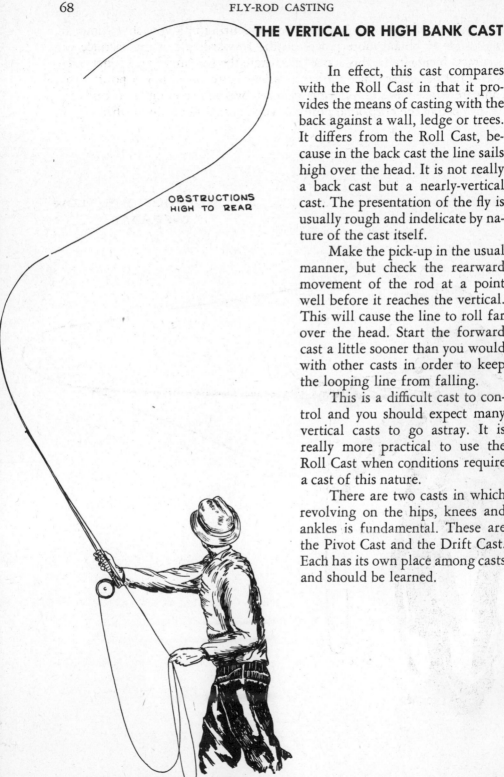

OBSTRUCTIONS
HIGH TO REAR

LEONARD

In effect, this cast compares with the Roll Cast in that it provides the means of casting with the back against a wall, ledge or trees. It differs from the Roll Cast, because in the back cast the line sails high over the head. It is not really a back cast but a nearly-vertical cast. The presentation of the fly is usually rough and indelicate by nature of the cast itself.

Make the pick-up in the usual manner, but check the rearward movement of the rod at a point well before it reaches the vertical. This will cause the line to roll far over the head. Start the forward cast a little sooner than you would with other casts in order to keep the looping line from falling.

This is a difficult cast to control and you should expect many vertical casts to go astray. It is really more practical to use the Roll Cast when conditions require a cast of this nature.

There are two casts in which revolving on the hips, knees and ankles is fundamental. These are the Pivot Cast and the Drift Cast. Each has its own place among casts and should be learned.

THE PIVOT CAST

The purpose of the pivot cast is to make possible a cast when you locate an opening among obstructions bordering the stream and you must make your back cast in that opening, regardless of its relationship to the forward cast. For example, if you are looking for sufficient space for your back cast, you may find that the only opening is to your right or left. In instances like this you must first determine where you will make the back cast and govern the pivoting of your body accordingly, while keeping in mind, at the same time, the final direction of the forward cast.

Face the body as nearly as possible at right angles to the place where the back cast and the fore cast will be made.

Turn your face in the direction you want to place the fly, while keeping in mind the position of the opening into which you will direct the back cast.

TARGET

WEIGHT ON RIGHT FOOT

LEONARD

Make a high vertical cast and swing the body on the hips, knees and ankles to observe and control the course of the line into the space you have assigned for the back cast.

TARGET

DIRECTION OF OPENING FOR BACK CAST

BODY PIVOTS ON HIPS AND ANKLES

WEIGHT ON LEFT FOOT

LEONARD

Before the line has fallen, immediately begin the return cast toward the final objective. Once again pivot on the hips, knees and ankles and direct the forward cast toward its target.

SLIGHT CROUCH AS BODY PIVOTS ON HIPS

TARGET

WEIGHT ON RIGHT FOOT

LEONARD

This cast is difficult to master. Your first attempts undoubtedly will end in failure. This is to be expected.

THE DRIFT CAST

The Drift Cast is merely a simple cast with the forward cast placed at right angles to the pick-up and back cast. The reason for its use is simple. Particularly when wet-fly fishing, it is effective to quarter the cast across stream and let the current sweep it downstream. Naturally you will not want to keep moving your position two or three times with every cast in order to follow the drift of the cast. The Drift Cast simplifies your problem.

Face cross-stream in the direction you plan to cast and place the fly. While the current sweeps the cast downstream, turn the upper part of your

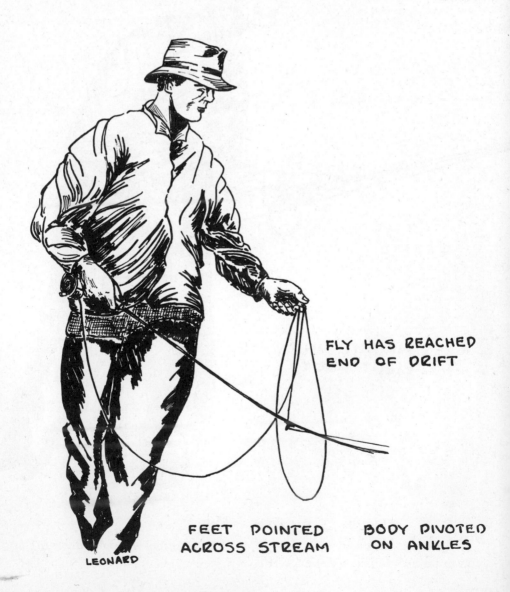

FLY HAS REACHED
END OF DRIFT

FEET POINTED   BODY PIVOTED
ACROSS STREAM   ON ANKLES

LEONARD

body in that direction. When the cast has run its course, make the pick-up in the conventional fashion or directly upstream and, when the back cast

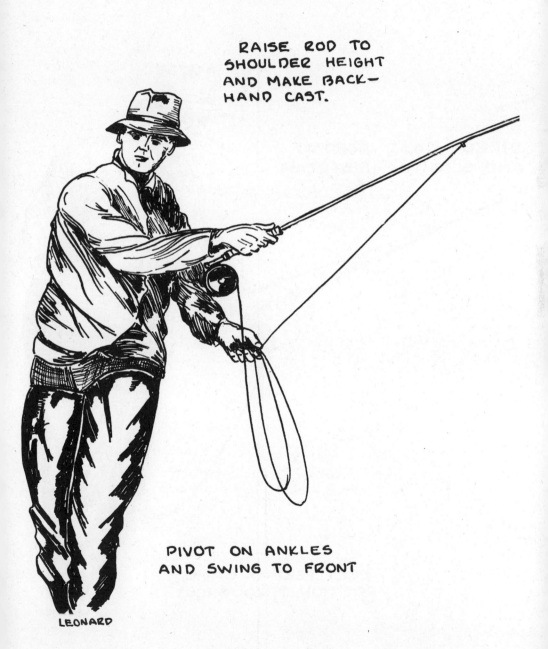

RAISE ROD TO
SHOULDER HEIGHT
AND MAKE BACK—
HAND CAST.

PIVOT ON ANKLES
AND SWING TO FRONT

LEONARD

has not quite extended its length, turn your body to face cross-stream again, making the forward cast in that same direction.

DIRECT CAST ACROSS
AND SLIGHTLY UPSTREAM

KEEP FEET IN SAME
POSITION THROUGHOUT

LEONARD

In rapid water, which often requires several casts through the same margin of water, the Drift Cast makes the repeated casts as tireless as possible. Co-ordination of the pick-up and back cast with the turning of the body and, finally, the forward cast, is the first consideration.

The chances are good that you have used this cast unknowingly, since the conditions which prompt its use are met frequently. Variations are numerous, but the principle is the same.

THE SNAP CAST

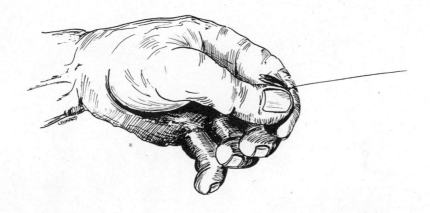

The Snap Cast is seldom used except on very small streams or from banks densely covered with brush and foliage. As the word implies, the cast is snapped in the same fashion that a sling shot snaps a stone. Care should be taken that the hook does not pierce the fingers, since the fly is held between the thumb and forefinger of the left hand, while the rod is arched. Aim is taken and the fly released to soar to the target. Naturally accuracy depends largely on the time and effort devoted to the mastering of this cast. It is best accomplished with wet flies and medium-weight leaders of short length.

OFFSETTING WIND AROUND THE CLOCK

Wind is, perhaps, the most unpredictable factor in planning smooth and delicate casting. On a few occasions it can be put to work, but don't depend on it. It is better to know how to overcome the effects of wind.

A wind to your left poses the problem of overcoming the force that tends to drive your forward cast to the right of its target. It calls for more

WIND

PICK-UP IN NEAR-
VERTICAL PLANE

LEONARD

FORWARD CAST QUARTERED
SLIGHTLY INTO WIND

power at the very beginning of the casting cycle. Pick up the line briskly to reduce the length of time the wind has a chance to alter its course behind you. Make a false cast or two to observe the effect of the wind on your forward cast. In every case make your pick-up or back cast with more power than usual. On the forward cast, using the knowledge the false casts have provided, power the line to the left of the target as much as seems necessary to drop the fly where you want it to be.

A wind to your right is a little more difficult to offset. Somewhat the same procedure applies here as for offsetting the left wind. Pick up your line cleanly and strongly, then drive it forward with more than usual power. Correction for drift of the line in the wind is made by inclining the forward cast toward the right after sensing with a false cast or two.

A head wind, or a wind to your front, often spoils a cast made with a long, light leader mainly because the fly offers so much resistance to the wind that it prevents the leader from straightening. Side loops such as are used to offset drag will be helpful here. This means a longer length of line than otherwise necessary (by actual measurement) and the forming of a loop on the water. (See page 81.)

STOP BACK-CAST SHORT

WIND

LEONARD

Another way to offset the effects of a head wind is to overcast the target and pull back with the rod tip to place the fly. This calls for some practice but has the advantage of keeping the floating line and leader more nearly aligned for strikes.

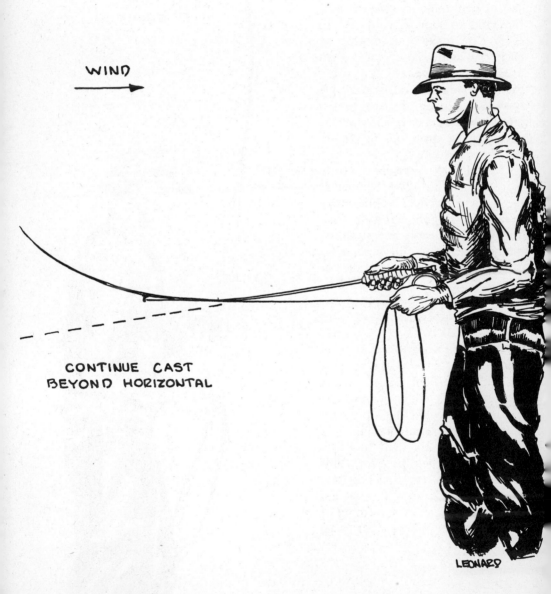

WIND

CONTINUE CAST
BEYOND HORIZONTAL

LEONARD

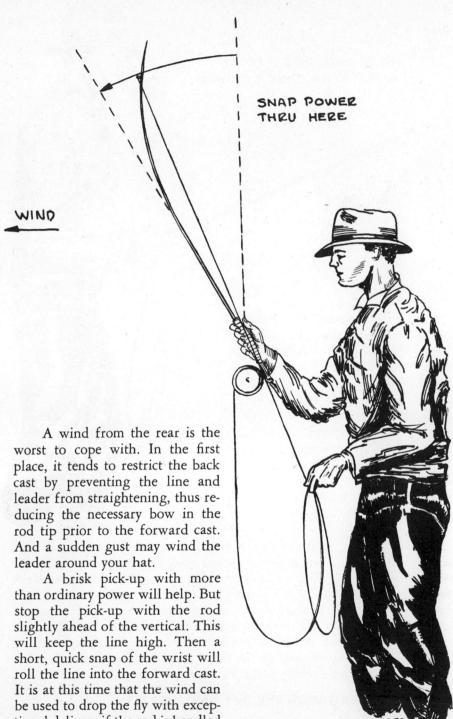

SNAP POWER
THRU HERE

WIND

A wind from the rear is the worst to cope with. In the first place, it tends to restrict the back cast by preventing the line and leader from straightening, thus reducing the necessary bow in the rod tip prior to the forward cast. And a sudden gust may wind the leader around your hat.

A brisk pick-up with more than ordinary power will help. But stop the pick-up with the rod slightly ahead of the vertical. This will keep the line high. Then a short, quick snap of the wrist will roll the line into the forward cast. It is at this time that the wind can be used to drop the fly with exceptional delicacy if the rod is handled well.

LEONARD

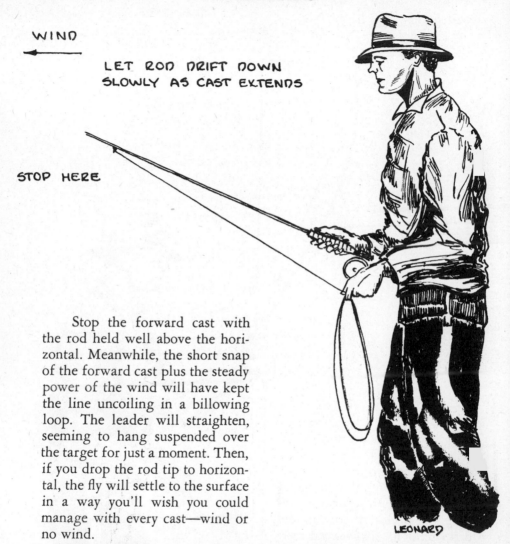

WIND

LET ROD DRIFT DOWN
SLOWLY AS CAST EXTENDS

STOP HERE

LEONARD

Stop the forward cast with the rod held well above the horizontal. Meanwhile, the short snap of the forward cast plus the steady power of the wind will have kept the line uncoiling in a billowing loop. The leader will straighten, seeming to hang suspended over the target for just a moment. Then, if you drop the rod tip to horizontal, the fly will settle to the surface in a way you'll wish you could manage with every cast—wind or no wind.

When slightly quartered to a back wind, it is possible to "steer" your cast after the driving power of the forward cast has been started. This is accomplished by dropping the tip slightly or pulling back. But watch the uncoiling of the curve on the forward cast. That is the guide to "steering." For example, if you are facing slightly to the right of the wind, the chances are the line and leader will be to the left of the fly, since the fly offers more resistance to the wind and is easily swept off course by it. Therefore, by pulling slightly, you will incline the fly to the left. The opposite applies when you are facing slightly to the left of the wind.

OFFSETTING DRAG WITH THE DRY AND WET FLY

Drag, that often-mentioned "bug" in everyone's casting, is a problem that will defy the best angler's tactics in many instances. It is the result of the leader spanning two or more sections of water traveling at different speeds. The fly may be in a panel of water hardly moving while two feet away the leader is caught in a surge of strong current. Naturally this pulls the fly across the quiet panel, or sinks it.

It is to be understood that no one formula exists for overcoming this condition. Every few feet the situation will vary. However, there are general methods for handling the rod which will allow the fly to remain just a little longer in a place likely to hold trout.

Since it is certain that a straight line and leader cannot eliminate drag, the only alternative is to cast a loop to allow the fly to rest until the faster-moving water has removed that loop and pulled the fly across or under.

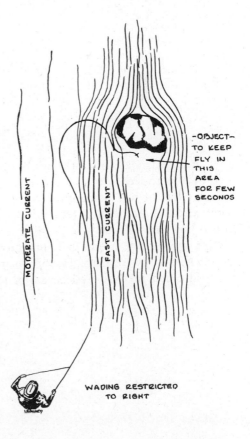

To cast this loop, you must flip the line beyond where you want the fly to settle so that the loop itself resembles a large hook with the fly becoming the hook point. What is sometimes called the Hook Cast is made this way. When making the forward cast, allow the coiled line held in the left hand (see pages 64 and 65 for proper technique) to shoot through the guides while the loop of the forward cast is still uncoiling. This will prevent the loop from straightening, resulting in the necessary hook. At first you will not be able to place the loop where you want it. But concentrate on its formation. Accuracy will develop with experience. Incidentally, a rear wind is ideal for casting these hooks.

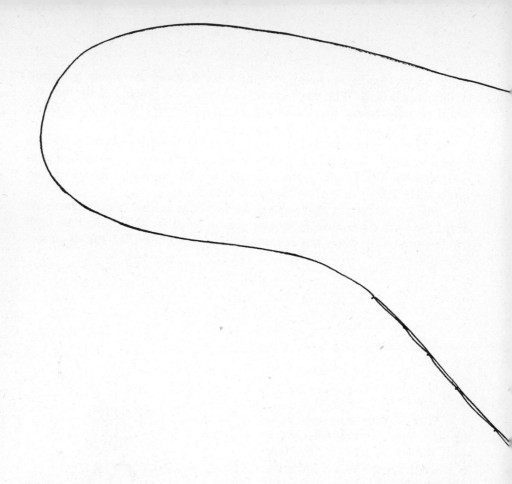

Another means of casting slack line consists of withholding the shooting of the coiled line in the left hand for just a moment longer than usual. Most of the momentum in the line will have become spent by this time and the momentum remaining will be sufficient only to pull a little more line through the guides. The leader, however, being light and impelled by the line alone, will not move forward with the line, with the result that a few serpentines will form slack near the end of the line.

The first method will be easier to learn.

RELEASE COILS IN
LEFT HAND BEFORE
LINE LOOP HAS STRAIGHT-
ENED OUT

LEONARD

FUNCTIONS OF THE LEFT HAND

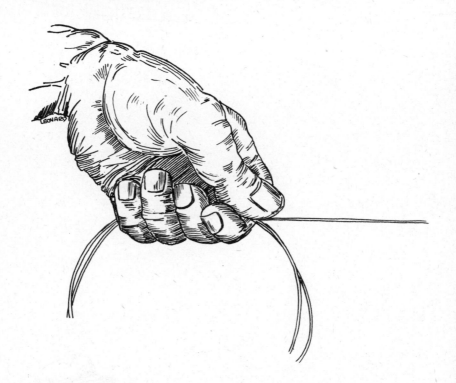

While actual casting is performed with the right hand, the functions of the left hand determine to no small degree the effectiveness of that casting. It is the left hand which times the shooting of the line on the forward cast. It adds extra power for long casts by stripping line through the guides while the rod is flexed with the load of starting the back cast. Let us examine these functions: shooting the line, releasing line on the back cast and extra-power casting. One, a combination of two, or a mixture of your own will create drive in your casts not realized with ordinary principles.

SHOOTING THE LINE

It is reasonable to assume that casting would be a tiring affair if every foot of line developed into the forward cast had to be withdrawn from the reel through a series of lengthened false casts. Furthermore, back casts cannot always be as long as the final forward casts due to foliage and shore conditions. Shooting the line, or letting the velocity of the line in the air pull additional feet of line held loosely coiled in the left hand, precludes many false casts. Try it this way.

Work out several rod lengths of line while casting smoothly. Then snub the line by placing it between the rod grasp and the index finger of

your right hand. While continuing to cast, strip three or four large loops of line from the reel, holding them between the thumb and forefinger of the left hand. On the next forward cast, which you should bring up briskly, let the loose coils shoot through the stripping guide but not until the velocity of the line itself has literally pulled the loops free. If you release the loops too soon, you will be casting a hook, which is not what you are after at this time. A good rule here is to wait until you see most of the line extended before you—then let go.

At first this may seem awkward. Your timing may be either too slow or too fast; but once you have experienced the feel of the cast and have seen the line shoot through the guides, you will slant toward accuracy immediately.

Shooting the line calls for well-greased line, good guides free from rough spots and, mainly, a line of proper weight for the flexure of your rod. Torpedo head or triple-diameter lines are especially good for shooting for distance. Quick taper lines such as these require an absolute minimum of false casts to shoot many feet of line. Remember, the whole thing stems from line velocity. A lazy forward cast will cause you grief. Chop your forward cast downward, preferably below the horizontal.

RELEASING LINE ON THE BACK CAST

One rapid way to increase line length is to let the looped line held in the left hand slip through the stripping guide during the back cast. This is possible when there is an unrestricted clearing for the back cast. This method is especially useful when casting into a head wind, since it reduces greatly the number of false casts necessary to produce an equal amount of line. For example, if fifteen feet of coiled line were held in the left hand and were to be released by making several false casts only, it would require at least two or three complete casting cycles to extend that fifteen feet. It is wise to hold the rod as high as convenient in the back cast, since a cast of this sort has the tendency to let the line fall more than it ordinarily would.

STRIPPING LINE FOR EXTRA POWER

Another device to add power and distance to your cast is stripping with the left hand during the beginning of the pick-up or back cast.

Look at it this way: since we have established that the forward cast is dependent upon the strength of the pick-up and back cast, we can assume that a back cast which is faster and more powerful than usual will result in a better forward cast. When you strip line with the left hand, you increase the load on the rod—hence, add to the rod flexure.

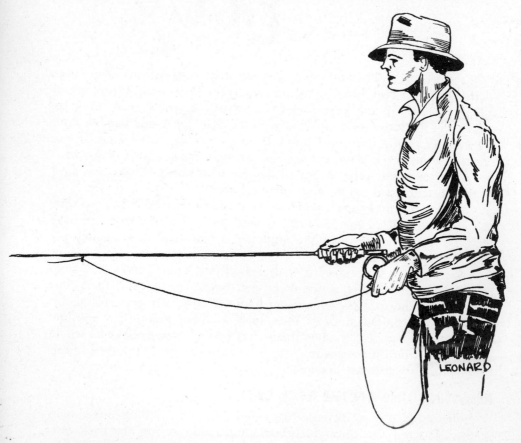

Pick up your rod and make a back cast. Notice that the length and weight of the line plus the snap of your wrist are the only reasons for any rod flexure at all. To increase the rod flexure, reach up close to the

REACH HIGH —
NEAR GUIDE

LEONARD

stripping guide with the thumb and forefinger of the left hand and swiftly pull back a full arm's length of line while the rod is bowed with the load of starting the pick-up. Rod bend will increase greatly. So will the velocity of the line speeding toward you.

PAUSE FOR TUG
ON BACKCAST

STRIP ARM'S
LENGTH FAST

LEONARD

Hold your arm high and wait for the tug on the rod indicating that
the line has sped its course on the back cast.

Then, with a downward sweep of the rod straighten your arm and drive the forward cast out in a steady flow of power.

When the line reaches far forward it will exert a definite pull on the line held in the left hand. Release this loop of line immediately and let it trail the leading portion to the end of the cast. Ideally, the tug and

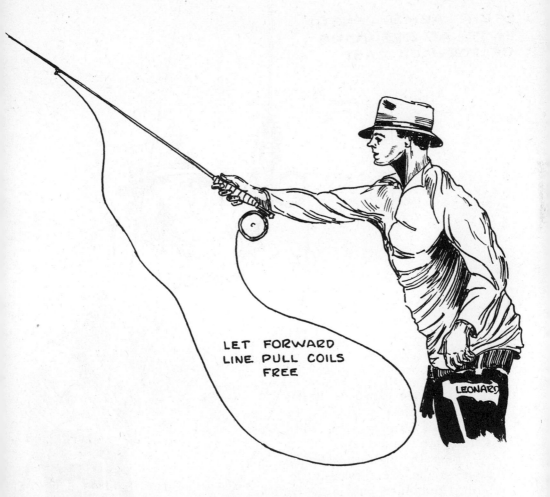

LET FORWARD
LINE PULL COILS
FREE

release of coiled line should be simultaneous to achieve the maximum distance. At first you will find the release will follow the tell-tale tug by a fraction; but keep trying to match that tug with an instantaneous release of the coiled line.

STRIP ARM'S LENGTH
FAST AT BEGINNING
OF FORWARD CAST

There are variations of this technique. Most useful is the method of stripping line when starting the forward cast.

Basically, the method is the same as the one previously described and differs only in the respect that the load is placed on the rod during the forward cast rather than on the pick-up or back cast. It accomplishes the same thing—longer, more powerful casts.

Learning to combine shooting the line with stripping on the back cast will make long casts less troublesome. Just one word of caution: Never overload a rod disproportionately. A rod has theoretical limits. It does not take long to recognize these after casting a short time with any rod.

A final suggestion for improving distance is the application of graphite to your line. It is rather messy—especially when handling flies. Otherwise it is a boon to the distance seeker.

INDEX